Best Easy D   D0678223

best
easy
day hikes

Colorado
Springs

Tracy Salcedo

GUILFORD, CONNECTICUT
HELENA, MONTANA

AN IMPRINT OF THE GLOBE PEQUOT PRESS

FALCONGUIDES®

Cover photo by Eric Wunrow.

ISBN 978-1-56044-853-2

Manufactured in the United States of America
First Edition/Ninth Printing

Contents

*This book is dedicated to all the Coloradans who have worked
to preserve wildlands throughout the state.*

Acknowledgments

This book would not have been possible without the help
of the kind strangers of Colorado Springs who offered their
advice on trail selection. I also would like to thank editor
Richard Chapman; Rick Ellsworth and Bryan G. Fons of
the USDA Forest Service, Pikes Peak Ranger District; John
Geerdes of Mueller State Park; Rich Havel and the El Paso
County Regional Parks system; Susan Smith, Interpretive
Ranger at Castlewood Canyon State Park; Harv Burman,
Seasonal Ranger at Florissant Fossil Beds National Monu-
ment; Gloria Wilson of the Colorado Parks and Recreation
Dept.; Nancy Salcedo; Chris Salcedo; George Meyers; hik-
ing pal (and more) Karen Charland; my beloved sons, Cruz,
Jesse and Penn; and my wonderful husband, Martin Chourré.

Map Legend

Interstate		Picnic Area	
U.S. Highway		Campground	▲
State or County Road		Bridge	
Interstate Highway		City Grid	
Paved Road			
Unpaved Road, Graded		Cabins/Buildings	■
Unpaved Road, Poor		Ranger Station	
Trailhead	○	Elevation	X 9,782 ft.
Main Trail		Mountain/Peak	
Secondary Trail		Falls, Pouroff	
Trailless Route		Pass/Saddle	)(
Large River		Gate	
River/Creek, Perennial		Map Orientation	N
Drainage, Intermittent Creek			
Spring	⌐	Scale	
Forest/Wilderness/ Park Boundary			0 30 60 Miles

Overview Map – The Plains

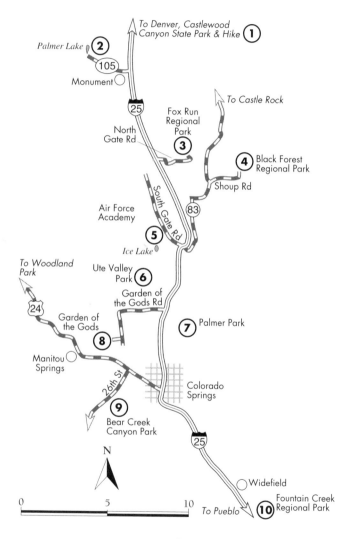

To Denver, Castlewood Canyon State Park & Hike (1)

Palmer Lake (2)

105

Monument

25

Fox Run Regional Park (3)

To Castle Rock

North Gate Rd

Black Forest Regional Park (4)

Shoup Rd

83

Air Force Academy

South Gate Rd

(5)

Ice Lake

To Woodland Park

24

Ute Valley Park (6)

Garden of the Gods Rd

Palmer Park (7)

Garden of the Gods (8)

Manitou Springs

26th St

Colorado Springs

(9)

Bear Creek Canyon Park

N

0   5   10

Widefield

25

Fountain Creek Regional Park (10)

To Pueblo

Overview Map – The Mountains

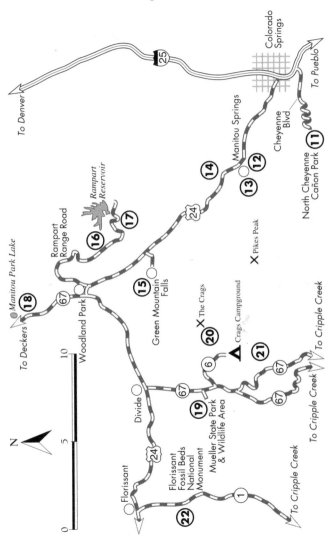

Ranking the Hikes

The following list ranks the hikes in this book from easiest to hardest.

Easiest

The Plains

Siamese Twins Trail
Fountain Creek Trail
Santa Fe Regional Trail at Ice Lake
Santa Fe Regional Trail at Palmer Lake
Coyote Gulch/Creekbottom Loop
Edna Mae Bennet Nature Trail
Fallen Timbers Loop
Ute Valley Park Loop
Black Forest Regional Park Loop

Hardest

Inner Canyon Loop

Easiest

The Mountains

BPW Nature Trail
Manitou Park Lake
Petrified Forest/Walk Through Time
Rainbow Gulch
Catamount Falls Trail
Paul Intemann Nature Trail
Mt. Cutler Trail
Outlook Ridge and Lost Pond Loop
Horsethief Falls
The Crags
Waldo Canyon Trail

Hardest

Lower Barr Trail

Introduction

"What is a best easy day hike?"

There is a widespread perception that great hikes exist primarily in national parks, forests, or wilderness areas. This is true, but it is also true that the favorite trails of most hikers are near to home. They are the trails walked on a Sunday afternoon with family, or on a summer evening after a hard day's work.

With this book and others like it, Falcon Publishing has allowed me to continue on a theme generated and brought to fruition when I worked as an author for Chockstone Press. Chockstone's *12 Short Hikes* series described short hikes—generally less than five miles long and two hours in duration—around major metropolitan areas and resort communities. The hikes were selected with the goal of expanding the horizons of visitors, area families, and local folk who were short on time, offering trails of varied length and atmosphere, all charming and all easy.

This guide to Colorado Springs was researched under the auspices of Chockstone and fostered under the care of Falcon Publishing. It represents the compilation of two *12 Short Hikes* guides—one to hikes on the plains that sweep eastward from the city, and one to treks in the stunning mountains that rise to the west. All the hikes pass within the shadow of Pikes Peak, the grand mountain that dominates the skyline from each route.

Easy, of course, is a relative term. Colorado Springs, even though it is at the edge of the high plains, is essentially a mountain town, and there are few hikes that don't involve at least some climbing. To aid in the selection of a hike that suits particular needs and abilities, I've ranked them from easiest to hardest. Bear in mind that even the steepest of these hikes can be made easy by hiking within your limits and taking rests when you need them. To approximate how long it will take you to complete a given trail, use the standard of two miles per hour, adding time if you are not a strong hiker or are traveling with small children, and subtracting time if you are an aerobic animal. Also add time for picnics, rest stops or other activities you plan for your outing.

To walk amid the grandeur of nature, whether along a narrow path that delves deeply into wilderness or on a well-kept paved trail lined with interpretive signs, is, I believe, to renew the soul. A guide to easy day hikes, like this one, suggests routes to that renewal, and has been compiled with the hope that anyone who embarks on a journey into the wild, regardless of its length, will find the peace and inspiration that I have found there.

- Tracy Salcedo

Zero Impact

While many of these hikes are so closely entwined with the urban environment that it may seem superfluous to advocate a "Zero Impact" philosophy, it is precisely because of their proximity to pollution and dense population that trail users and advocates must be especially vigilant to leave no lasting mark. Many of these trails lie in parks that are enclaves of wildness in the metropolis, and only by practicing the same care and consideration that we do in wilderness areas can we preserve the parks as natural areas.

Equate traveling these trails to visiting a museum. You obviously avoid leaving marks on art treasures in the museum. If everyone who visited the museum left one tiny mark, the art would be destroyed—and what would a big building full of trashed art be worth? The same goes for the trails of Colorado Springs. If we all leave just one little mark on the landscape, the parks and wildlands will soon be despoiled.

These trails can accommodate plenty of human travel as long as everyone treats them with respect. Just a few thoughtless, badly mannered, or uninformed visitors can ruin them for everyone who follows. The book *Leave No Trace* is a valuable resource for learning more about these principles.

Three Falcon Principles of Zero Impact

- *Leave with everything you brought with you.*
- *Leave no sign of your visit.*
- *Leave the landscape as you found it.*

Litter is the scourge of all trails. It is unsightly, polluting, and potentially dangerous to wildlife. Pack out all your garbage, and while you're at it, consider packing out trash left by less considerate hikers.

Don't approach or feed the wildlife—the deer begging for your snack food is best able to survive if it is self-reliant.

Please, don't pick the wildflowers—leave them for the next hiker to enjoy. The same goes for rocks, antlers, feathers and other treasures you see along the trail. Not only will removing these items take away from the next hiker's experience, it also may violate park regulations.

Remain on the established route to avoid damaging trailside soils and plants. Don't cut switchbacks, which can promote erosion; leaving the trail also may mean trampling fragile vegetation, especially at altitude. Select durable surfaces like rocks, logs, or sandy spots for rests.

Many of these trails are multi-use, which means you'll share them with other hikers, trail runners, mountain bikers and equestrians. Familiarize yourself with the proper etiquette, yielding the trail when appropriate. Be courteous by not making loud noises while hiking.

If possible, use outhouses at trailheads or along the trail. If not, pack in a lightweight trowel and a plastic bag so that you can bury your waste 6 to 8 inches deep and pack out used toilet paper. Make sure you are at least 300 feet away from any surface water or boggy spot when you go.

Zero impact—put your ear to the ground and listen carefully. Thousands of people coming behind you are thankful for your courtesy and good sense.

Be Prepared

Generally, hiking in Colorado Springs is safe and fun, but you must exercise caution as well as your legs. There is much you can do to ensure each outing is safe and enjoyable. I encourage all hikers to verse themselves completely in the science of backcountry travel—it's knowledge worth having and it's easy to acquire.

Some specific advice:

Know the basics of first aid, including how to treat bleeding, bites, stings, fractures, strains, and sprains. None of these hikes are so remote that help can't be reached within a short time, but you'd be wise to carry and know how to use simple supplies like over-the-counter pain relievers, bandages, and ointments. Pack a first aid kit on each excursion.

Familiarize yourself with the symptoms and treatment of altitude sickness (especially if you are visiting the area from a significantly lesser altitude). If you or one of your party exhibits any symptom of this potentially fatal condition, including headache, nausea, and unusual fatigue seek medical attention.

Know the symptoms of both cold- and heat-related conditions, including hypothermia and heat stroke. The best way to avoid these afflictions is to wear appropriate clothing, drink lots of water, eat enough to keep the internal fires properly stoked and keep a pace within your physical limits.

Be prepared for the vagaries of Colorado weather. It changes in a heartbeat. The sun can be brutal, so wear a strong sunscreen. Afternoon and evening thunderstorms, while spectacular, harbor a host of potential hazards, including rain, hail, and lightning. Retreat to the safety of the car or other shelter if you suspect the weather will turn, and carry protective clothing.

Keep children under careful watch. Waterways move deceptively fast, animals and plants may harbor danger, and rocky terrain and cliffs are potential hazards. Children should carry a plastic whistle; if they become lost, they should stay in one place and blow the whistle to summon help.

You'll enjoy each of these hikes much more if you wear good socks and hiking boots. Carry a comfortable backpack loaded with water, snacks and extra clothing, including a warm hat, gloves, a jacket, and the appropriate maps. Pack a camera, binoculars, or a good novel to curl up with on a warm rock if that will heighten your enjoyment of the hike.

The Plains

Arguably the most spectacular peak in the Colorado
Rockies, Pikes Peak feels particularly massive because of its
proximity to the High Plains. Its barren summit rises directly from the gold and green prairie that rolls away to the
east, casting a beautiful and forbidding presence over the
picturesque city of Colorado Springs.

Each of the trails described in this guide offers great views
of Pikes Peak—indeed, it's tough to find a place in "the
Springs" that doesn't offer such a view. But the hikes that
follow have other charms as well. In the Garden of the Gods,
spectacular red-rock formations form a frame for western
vistas. Along Fountain Creek, stately elms and cottonwoods
offer shady respite. On trails that wind through the grasslands, an abundance of wildflowers that bloom in succession throughout the spring and summer—purple pentstemon, gaudy Indian paintbrush, delicate crocus, and vibrant
wallflower—dance in the breezes that flow over the shoulders of the grand mountain to the west.

The hikes in this section of the guide lie on the rolling
plains east of the foothills. The hikes are listed from north
to south along Interstate 25 and none take longer than an
hour to reach from the heart of Colorado Springs.

1
INNER CANYON LOOP

Type of hike: Loop.
Total distance: 2 miles.
Elevation loss: 200 feet.
Jurisdiction: Castlewood Canyon State Park.
Maps: USGS Russelville Gulch and Castle Rock South.
Starting point: Canyon Point trailhead in Castlewood Canyon State Park.
Finding the trailhead: To reach Castlewood Canyon State Park and the trailhead, take Interstate 25 north from Colorado Springs to the Wilcox Street/Plum Creek Parkway exit (Exit 181) in Castle Rock. Take Wilcox St. east 0.9 mile to a right onto Fifth/Colorado Highway 86 to Franktown. Go east 7 miles on CO 86 to Colorado Highway 83 in Franktown. Go right (south) on CO 83 for 5.2 miles to the park entrance. Turn right (west) and go 0.5 mile to the entrance/fee station; there is a fee. Drive 0.5 mile to the trailhead parking at Canyon Point. The Canyon View Nature Trail and Inner Canyon Trail share the trailhead on the northeast side of the lot.

Key points:
0.4   Reach the canyon bottom
1.2   Turn left on the Lake Gulch Trail
1.7   Pause to look at Pikes Peak at the overlook

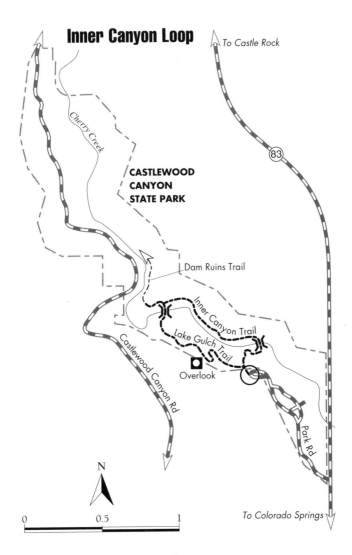

Inner Canyon Loop

To Castle Rock

Cherry Creek

CASTLEWOOD CANYON STATE PARK

83

Dam Ruins Trail

Inner Canyon Trail

Lake Gulch Trail

Castlewood Canyon Rd

Overlook

Park Rd

N

0   0.5   1

To Colorado Springs

9

The hike: Castlewood Canyon is a startling gouge in the prairie. Deceptively placid most of the year, the relentless and occasionally furious flow of Cherry Creek has carved this steep shallow gorge, exposing the tan and gray rock that underlays the grassland. The canyon cliffs are an ideal playground for rock climbers, who splay colorfully above the trails. At creekside, sun-splashed rocks shelter pools in which hikers can cool their heels after rambling about in the sunbaked canyon bottom.

Follow the paved path through picnic sites to the Inner Canyon Trail proper. Veer left (west) onto the dirt track amidst scrub oak. Stairs drop quickly down the canyon wall to a bridge spanning Cherry Creek. Cross the bridge (0.4 mile) and go left (southwest).

The rustic path continues its streamside traverse, eventually crossing two more bridges, the second near a huge dead pine. Beyond, the route climbs above the creek, with brief exposure, to stairs that return you to the creek's edge. Drop around boulders to a bridge with rails and stone steps.

The trail gradually descends to an intersection with the Lake Gulch Trail and the Dam Ruins Trail (1.2 miles). Turn left (south) on Lake Gulch Trail, crossing the bridge and traversing up through the meadow and out of the canyon. The trail circumnavigates the dry slope to views of a pastoral valley. At the overlook (1.7 miles), check out Pikes Peak, which looms majestically on the southwest horizon.

Put the silvery ramparts of the Front Range to your back as you continue up and left (east) to the flat rim of the canyon and wander through the waving grasses to the picnic area and parking lot (2 miles).

2
SANTA FE REGIONAL TRAIL
AT PALMER LAKE

Type of hike: Out-and-back.
Total distance: 4 miles.
Elevation gain/loss: Minimal.
Maps: USGS Palmer Lake, Trails Illustrated Pikes Peak/Cañon City.
Starting point: Palmer Lake Regional Recreation Area.
Finding the trailhead: To reach the Palmer Lake trailhead, go north on Interstate 25 to the Palmer Lake exit (Exit 161). Go left (west) over the freeway, then stay west (right) on Colorado Highway 105. Follow CO 105 for 4 miles, through the town of Palmer Lake, to County Line Road. Go right (east) on County Line Road for 0.1 mile to the Palmer Lake Regional Recreation Area, part of the El Paso County Regional Parks system. Park in the lot at the end of the road. The trailhead is at the southern edge of the parking lot.

Key points:
1.0   Pass Ben Lomand Mountain
2.0   Reach the turnaround point

The hike: The Santa Fe Regional Trail sits atop the raised bed of the old Atchison, Topeka and Santa Fe Railroad. Nearby are modern railroad tracks, upon which diesel locomotives travel north to Denver and south to Colorado

Springs and beyond. Though not a wilderness experience, the thunderous approach of a train in such proximity evokes noisy images of nineteenth-century locomotive travel across the wilderness that once was the American West.

A hike along this easy multi-use trail plunges you into the history of both of the railroad and the quaint town of

Santa Fe Regional Trail at Palmer Lake

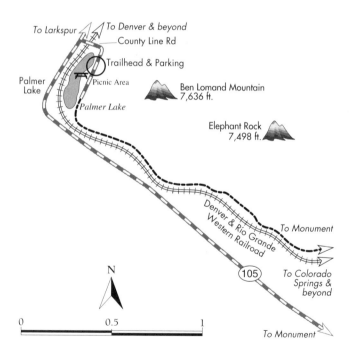

Palmer Lake, which was known for a time as the "Switzerland of America."

The trail begins by skirting the still waters of Palmer Lake, which is sheltered by large shade trees. At the south end of the lake the trail forks; go left (southeast) on the broad path. A berm shelters both sides of the route.

Round a bend in the trail and views open far and away to the south. Pass an interpretive sign on old-time wildflower-picking excursions, then another on Colorado's state flower, the columbine, and watch the orange cliffs to the north and west for signs of raptors.

The path arcs eastward between berms and evergreens. Pass a sign describing Ben Lomand Mountain, the one-mile marker, then signs that discuss Elephant Rock and logging. Meadows laden with summertime wildflowers stretch to the north at breaks in the bordering berm.

The farther south and east you travel on this broad trail, the more sheltered you are from urban sounds and signs. Prairie and woodland intermingle, with the dark hump of the Black Forest on the eastern horizon. Continue past more interpretive signs, including one on the stately vanilla-scented ponderosa pine.

Homes encroach on the trail just past the two-mile marker. You can continue to the town of Monument, and beyond, but this is a natural stopping point. Retrace your steps to the trailhead.

3
FALLEN TIMBERS LOOP

Type of hike: Loop.
Total distance: 2 miles.
Elevation gain: 165 feet.
Jurisdiction: El Paso County Regional Parks.
Maps: USGS Monument, El Paso County Regional Parks pamphlet.
Starting point: Fallen Timbers trailhead in Fox Run Regional Park.
Finding the trailhead: To reach Fox Run Regional Park, take Interstate 25 to the Gleneagle Drive exit (Exit 156A). Turn right (east), following the sign, onto North Gate Road. Go east 3.0 miles on North Gate Road to Rollercoaster Road. Go left (north) on Rollercoaster for 1.5 miles to Stella Drive. Go left (west) on Stella for 0.3 mile to the park entrance. Turn right (north) into the park, and drive 0.1 mile to the T intersection; go left (northwest), and follow the road 0.8 mile to the Fallen Timbers parking area. The trailhead is on the west side of the parking loop.

Key points:
0.5   Crest the first hill
1.0   Cross the bridge to the orange-blazed trail

The hike: The sunlight that filters through the dense canopy of ponderosa pine imparts an atmosphere of warmth and shelter to this easy wilderness route. The trail wanders through thick forest, gently climbing and falling along ridges, with Pikes Peak making cameo appearances at breaks in the wall of trees. Interpretive signs help you understand this gentle, vanilla-scented ecosystem.

From the trailhead, the broad, sandy path rambles into the woods to a trail fork. Go up and right (northwest). Pass a cluster of interpretive signs about the pine beetle; a fence forces the ascending trail to bend right (east).

Fallen Timbers Loop

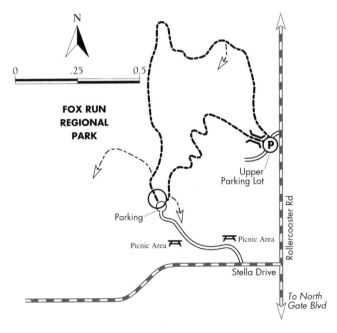

The trail mellows beyond the crest of the hill (0.5 mile), and you'll rollercoaster in and out of gullies. An easy descent leads past another fence to two interpretive signs about tree bores. Just beyond is a trail intersection. Go straight (left/east), and continue the gentle descent, enjoying more interpretive signs as you drop to the parking area for the upper trailhead. Go right (southwest), crossing the bridge and begin a gentle climb. Orange blazes mark the route (1.0 mile).

The top of the hill is marked by a sign about lightning. Pikes Peak is visible to the west. Go left (south), along the ridge-top. The next cluster of interpretive signs (about dwarf mistletoe) marks the trail's departure from the ridge. At about 1.5 miles, you'll reach the next trail crossing; go straight (left/west) and begin an easy climb past more interpretive signs.

Reach a second ridge top and go left, walking along its spine. A picnic table sits on a wooded knoll at the next trail intersection. Go right (west), back to the parking area (2.0 miles).

Options: The Fallen Timbers loop trail is but one of the amenities you'll find at Fox Run Regional Park. After your hike, take the kids to the playground, have a picnic by the shores of Aspen or Spruce Lakes, play on one of the ballfields, or pick up a game of volleyball.

4
BLACK FOREST
REGIONAL PARK LOOP

Type of hike: Loop.
Total distance: Approx. 2.2 miles.
Elevation gain: 190 feet.
Jurisdiction: El Paso County Regional Parks.
Maps: USGS Black Forest, El Paso County Regional Parks pamphlet.
Starting point: West edge of upper parking area in Black Forest Regional Park.
Finding the trailhead: To reach Black Forest Regional Park, take the South Academy exit (Exit 150). Go east on Academy Blvd. for 0.2 mile to the first stoplight, at Colorado Highway 83. Turn left onto CO 83 and drive 5.2 miles north to Shoup Road. Go right (east) on Shoup Road for 2.3 miles to Milam Road and turn left (north). Drive 0.2 mile on Milam Road to the upper parking lot.

Key points:
1.0   Reach a three-way trail crossing at the top of the hill
1.5   Hike down along the rolling trail
2.0   Reach the orange-blazed trail

The hike: Envision an oasis of a different kind. In the midst of the sun-scorched prairie, within sight of a great mountain range but still quite distant, a shady forest grows. Ponderosa pine are spread on the land with a parklike neatness, allowing enough sun to reach the forest floor for kinnikinnick and purple pentstemon to flourish. At high points, you can see the rolling green plains to the east, and the white-streaked massif of Pikes Peak to the west. This is the Black Forest, a wonderful splash of woodland amid the prairie grasses.

Like the Fox Run park complex (Hike 3), Black Forest offers more than just hiking: you can mountain bike, picnic and set the kids free at the playground or on the large grassy playing field. The trails were not marked when this hike was researched, but a series of colored blazes stained the trees. Don't fret the lack of signs; it is relatively easy to find a trail that loops back to the parking area.

To begin, head directly east from the parking lot. This route, generally the broadest, is intersected by a series of smaller, less formal trails. At the first trail fork, go left (northeast), following the blue blazes. Crest a rise; at the next trail crossing, go left (north), now following orange blazes. The sandy path rolls to another Y intersection. Stay left (straight/north). Reach yet another trail intersection; stay left again (ever northward), following the orange blazes and the pictures of cross-country skiers on the trees.

Reach a four-way trail crossing at a split log-sided shelter. Go straight (north), passing behind the shelter and staying with the orange blazes. A steady climb leads to yet another trail intersection at the top of the hill (1.0 mile). Go left (west), toward the mountains, passing a wind-washed pine with a commanding view of Pikes Peak. Stay straight on the broad path, ignoring side trails on the short descent. At the bottom of the hill, make a sharp left (south) on the rolling trail, which dips in and out of drainages but continues its downward trend (1.5 miles).

The trail loops on a wide switchback to a gentle uphill section. This links up with an orange-blazed trail at the trail intersection (2 miles). Go right (south/down), dropping back toward the parking area. Stay left (southeast) at the fork, following the orange blazes to the trailhead (2.2 miles).

Black Forest Regional Park Loop

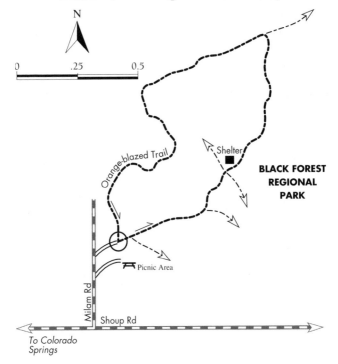

5
SANTA FE REGIONAL TRAIL
AT ICE LAKE

Type of hike: Out-and-back.
Total distance: 4 miles.
Elevation gain: 100 feet.
Jurisdiction: El Paso County Regional Parks.
Maps: USGS Pikeview, Trails Illustrated Pikes Peak/Cañon City.
Starting point: Ice Lake trailhead in the U.S. Air Force Academy.
Finding the trailhead: To reach the Ice Lake trailhead from Interstate 25, take the South Academy exit (Exit 150). Go left (west) on South Gate Road into the U.S. Air Force Academy. After 2.8 miles, turn left (west) onto Pine Drive. Go 0.4 mile on Pine Drive, then turn left (south) onto an unmarked dirt road. Go 0.9 miles, crossing the railroad tracks, to the parking area. Give yourself some extra time to complete this route, or check the railroad schedule beforehand, because the trains that roll through the area have been known to hold hikers hostage in the parking area for up to a hour. Provided you don't have a pressing engagement, this should not pose a problem; it is tough to find a more beautiful place to cultivate idle time.

Santa Fe Regional Trail at Ice Lake

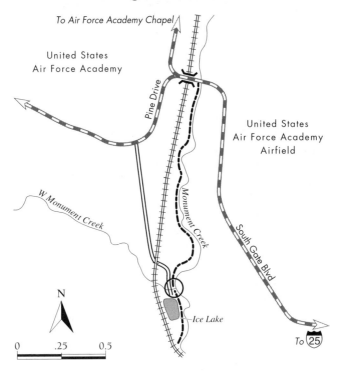

Key points:

0.5   Reach the end of the canyon

1.5   Ramble through the meadow

2.5   Trail's end at the South Gate Road bridge

The hike: The Air Force Academy owns some of the most scenic real estate in Colorado Springs. This section of the Santa Fe Regional Trail passes through relatively undeveloped academy property, once again following the abandoned bed of the Atchison, Topeka and Santa Fe Railroad. Ice Lake serves as the trailhead, from which you can hike south into a small gray-rock canyon, or north into the broad meadows and riparian habitats that line Monument Creek. Either way, you'll enjoy spectacular views of the Front Range as you hike.

The Air Force Academy has granted access to this section of the 14-mile long Santa Fe Trail with the condition that hikers and other users don't leave the designated route. The path, though dirt, is flat and well maintained, and is suitable for wheelchairs.

Trail sections head both to the south and north of Ice Lake. You can choose to hike one way or the other, or combine them as described below for a longer trek.

To begin, walk to the right (south) from the parking lot, passing the park sign. Groves of cottonwood and willow shade the trail to the first interpretive sign, which describes ice ponds. Continue south, passing below the grassy levees that contain Ice Lake.

Beyond the lake, pass a second interpretive sign on floods, and listen for the frogs that populate the peaceful dell throughout the hiking season. The trail curves into the wrinkled gray-walled canyon. The rusted remnants of a bridge poke from the waters of the creek. The trail ends just beyond the border of the canyon (0.5 mile). Turn around and head back as you came.

To explore the meadowlands north of Ice Lake, continue past the parking area on the flat, wide path. Weathered silvering cliffs line the bank on the opposite side of the creek. Pass an interpretive sign that describes the sounds of the meadow and, in spring and summer, pause to listen to the crickets and frogs perform a raucous symphony amid the grasses.

Wander away from the creek onto high prairie (1.5 miles), and pass a mile marker as you crest a hillock. A couple of interpretive signs, one on harvester ants and another discussing riparian habitat, decorate the trail before it dips into a gully.

Ramble on through the grassland to the shade of a large, lonely cottonwood; farther along, you will cross a culvert. The South Gate bridge, which spans both creek and railroad tracks, also is the structure on which a multitude of swallows have built their nests. The brown cones are tucked under its concrete eaves, and the birds flicker to and from like little whirlwinds. The 13-mile marker lies just beyond (2.5 miles).

The bridge is the turnaround point, but you can continue if you desire; the trail rambles north to Monument and beyond. Otherwise, retrace your steps back to the parking area and trailhead.

6
UTE VALLEY PARK LOOP

Type of hike: Loop.
Total distance: 2.5 miles.
Elevation gain: 120 feet.
Maps: USGS Pikeview, Trails Illustrated Pikes Peak/Cañon City.
Starting point: Parking area off Vindicator Drive.
Finding the trailhead: To reach Ute Valley Park from Interstate 25, take the Rockrimmon Blvd. exit (Exit 147). Go west on Rockrimmon Blvd. for 1.5 miles to Vindicator Drive. Turn left (west) on Vindicator, and drive 0.7 mile. Turn left (south) into the small parking lot.

Key points:
1.0   Reach the overlook rock
1.4   Cross the foot bridge
2.0   Crest the top of the last hill

The hike: Though surrounded by the suburban sprawl of Colorado Springs, the craggy, sparsely forested bluffs and narrow, nameless trails of Ute Valley Park insulate hikers, mountain bikers, and trail runners from the concrete and asphalt of encroaching subdivisions.

You'll find yourself cradled in a haven of shallow draws and climbing hillsides draped in sun-bleached grasses and wildflowers. At the high points of the circuitous route described here, you'll entertain views of both Pikes Peak and the city that sprawls at its feet. The juxtaposition is striking and thought-provoking. But, no doubt amid the observa-

Ute Valley Park Loop

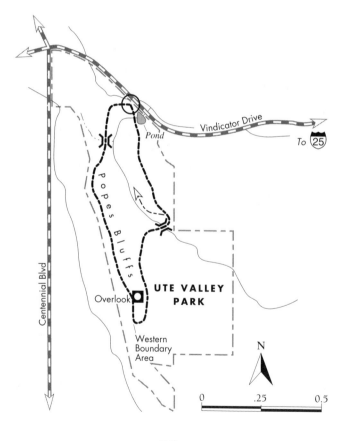

tions you might make about the contrasting environments, you'll thank the powers-that-be for preserving the juniper-studded wildland of Popes Bluffs. The stark rock outcroppings and the sharp-walled canyon that cradles the stream surely deserve preservation.

Upon departing from the trailhead at the southeast corner of the parking lot, you'll pass a small pond. At the trail fork, go right (southwest) into a sparsely wooded area. At the next trail crossing, go straight (south). Another intersection; stay left (southeast), walking into a sheltered valley. Ignore side trails; shortly, you will cross a bridge over a seasonal stream.

The route begins a traversing climb up the southern wall of a steepening and narrowing canyon. Eventually the trail flattens as it traverses along the canyon rim, climbing gently over blonde slabs to a trail crossing at the top of the hill.

The main route continues straight; a foot path branches off to the flat-topped overlook on the left (1.0 mile). Visit the viewpoint, then return to the main trail, which begins a gentle descent to a parking area and sign at the western boundary of the park. Make a sharp switchback to the left (north) and continue down. At the trail crossing, stay straight (left/north). Drop into a gully and a trail crossing; go left (northwest).

Shortly, you'll reach a series of small trail crossings. You'll bear northwest at all of the intersections: At the first, go left (uphill). At the next, go straight. At the third, stay left. Negotiate a steep hump at the fourth fork and head downhill. When you reach the valley floor, pass a split rail fence and yet another couple of trail crossings. Stay left (up the valley), and cross the foot bridge (1.4 miles).

At the next trail fork, go right (north), ignoring the trail sign. Climb the rocky knoll, staying straight (right/northwest) where side trails beckon. Crest the yucca-crowned knoll (2.0 miles) and follow the path along the ridge top. Pass a revegetation sign and drop back past the small pond to the parking area.

Options: As the description above indicates, there are a number of trails that wind through this park. If you've the time and inclination, explore these varied and entertaining paths. You can't go wrong—the park's just not big enough!

7
EDNA MAE BENNET NATURE TRAIL

Type of hike: Loop.
Total distance: 1.8 miles.
Elevation gain: 130 feet.
Maps: USGS Pikeview, Trails Illustrated Pikes Peak/Cañon City.
Jurisdiction: Palmer Park.
Starting point: North Cañon trailhead in Palmer Park.
Finding the trailhead: To reach the trailhead from Interstate 25, take the Fillmore St. exit (Exit 145). Go east on Fillmore (which becomes N. Circle Drive beyond the Union Blvd. intersection) for 2.5 miles to Paseo Road. Go left (north) on Paseo for 0.8 miles, passing the golf course. Turn left immediately after passing through the gated entrance and park in the lot at the North Canyon Trailhead.

Key points:
0.8   Reach the first rail intersection
1.3   Pass the amphitheater and cave on the descent
1.8   Stairs drop into trailhead parking lot

The hike: The interface between the urban expanse of Colorado Springs and the wilderness of the foothills below Pikes Peak is abrupt, and is illustrated with startling clarity from the rimrock apex of the Edna Mae Bennet Nature Trail.

Edna Mae Bennet Nature Trail

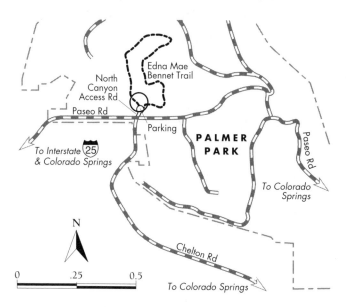

The trail is relatively rustic. It meanders through the drab scrub of a seasonal streambed before climbing to the edge of the pine-studded yellow sandstone canyon. The rocks of the canyon walls have been puckered and scoured by rainfall and snowmelt, but offer wonderful opportunities for you and your children to do some low-key clambering and for all to rest upon while enjoying the views.

The trailhead is marked by a huge sign dedicating the trail to the memory of Edna Mae Bennet, a schoolteacher who developed a nature-based curriculum for area children.

The gently climbing path leads along rustic split-rail fences through fragrant brush. Mount the stairs and cross the seasonal stream. At the trail fork, stay right (up/northeast) on the main path. Climb a stone staircase past a mushroom-shaped rock.

Two switchbacks lead to a trail crossing (0.8 mile). Stay right (southwest) on the Bennet Trail and continue to climb. The trail levels and traverses for a stretch just below the rim of the canyon, then climbs to the top, all the while revealing a stunning panorama of Colorado Springs and Pikes Peak.

The descent begins with a switchback; pass a metal post marked with a white arrow that points the way. At the next trail post, follow the Bennet Trail right (west) and downward. The route switches back; a little rock garden to the left (east) of the curve forms a kind of natural amphitheater and includes a shallow cave (1.3 miles).

The trail flattens at the base of a white rock wall. Go straight (right/northwest) and up over "bars" set in the trail to discourage erosion. The route's traverse along the lower canyon is intersected by mini-arroyos. Arrows point the way.

Some balanced rocks and a short set of stairs drop you back to a flat trail heading south to the trailhead (1.8 miles).

Options: A dollop of wilderness preserved in the midst of the city, Palmer Park offers many other hiking opportunities, as well as mountain biking and picnicking. Explore!

8
SIAMESE TWINS TRAIL

Type of hike: Loop.
Total distance: 0.5 mile.
Elevation gain: 150 feet.
Maps: USGS Colorado Springs and Cascade, Trails Illustrated Pikes Peak/Cañon City.
Jurisdiction: Garden of the Gods Park.
Starting point: Spring Canyon in Garden of the Gods Park.
Finding the trailhead: To reach the Garden of the Gods from Interstate 25, take the Garden of the Gods Road exit (Exit 146). Drive west on Garden of the Gods for 2.1 miles to 30th Street. Turn left (south) on 30th, and drive 1.4 miles to the park entrance (Gateway Road), which is opposite the park's Visitor Center. Turn right (west) on Gateway Road, which becomes Juniper Way Loop as you circle the Gateway Rocks, and go 1 mile to where the road splits. Veer right (southwest) on Garden Drive for 0.9 mile to the Spring Canyon trailhead. Turn right (northwest) at the Spring Canyon trailhead, and go 0.1 mile to the parking lot.

Key points:
0.3   Reach the Siamese Twins

The hike: A stay in Colorado Springs without a visit to Garden of the Gods Park would be like eating an ice cream sundae without a cherry on top—it's yummy, but you know something's missing.

Siamese Twins Trail

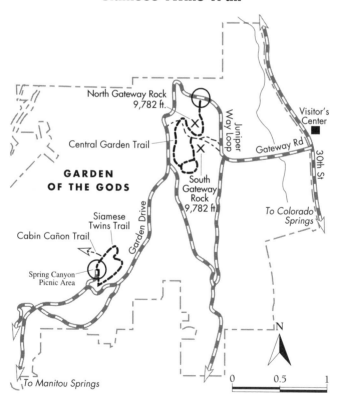

A variety of hiking opportunities are available in this spectacular park. The Siamese Twins Trail described here is one of the easy trails less travelled, which, coupled with the truly remarkable views seen from Twins, makes it a true gem.

The oval opening chiseled by wind and water into the Siamese Twins formation frames a perfect picture of Pikes Peak. Clamber into this smooth-bottomed window and your eyes can't help but be drawn to the stunning massif that barricades the western horizon. Nature's brilliant palette—the faded garnet of the Garden's rock, the deep emerald of the blanketing conifer forest and the pearly white of the peak's summit—is most vivid in spring.

The trailhead is at the north (upper) end of the parking area. Climb the trail alongside the split rail fence. Pass the Cabin Cañon Trail on the left (west); stay right (north) on the Siamese Twins Trail and climb a set of stairs. The trail follows a red rock draw amid scrub oak and juniper.

A second set of broad stairs leads to the bed of a seasonal stream, which is forded via a dirt bridge built on a culvert. The trail continues up toward lumps of red rock. Drop across the draw again, and circle southeast toward the twin sentinel rocks. Spiny yucca lines the climb. Pass a trail marker and bear left (south), ascending to great views amid the Twins and their smaller brothers and sisters (0.3 mile). Recline on a slab of sun-warmed rock and let your gaze wander from the red formations that are spread along the foothills to Pikes Peak above.

To descend to the trailhead, circle around to the west side of the formation and rejoin the trail at the trail marker; go left (south). Pass a second trail marker at the base of a great slab of red rock, and walk beside a log fence. The winding path takes you down along the spine of a small ridge, then along a second log fence to yet another trail marker. Go right (west).

At the last trail junction, stay right (west). It's a quick hop down some stairs to the parking lot (0.5 mile).

Options: The Siamese Twins Trail can be done in conjunction with one of the longer trails that laces through the red rock architecture. Refer to the park brochure, available at the visitor center, for details.

The flat, paved, wheelchair-accessible Central Garden Trail is the quintessential hike in this famous rock garden, threading between the sheer red, orange and pink faces of the North and South Gateway Rocks. The parking area and trailhead are just off the Juniper Way Loop—you can't miss them.

9
COYOTE GULCH/
CREEKBOTTOM LOOP

Type of hike: Loop.
Total distance: 2 miles.
Elevation gain: 140 feet.
Jurisdiction: Bear Creek Regional Park and Nature Center.
Maps: USGS Colorado Springs, Trails Illustrated Pikes Peak/
Cañon City.
Starting point: Bear Creek Nature Center parking area.
Finding the trailhead: To reach the trailhead from Interstate
25, take the Cimarron St./US Highway 24 exit (Exit 141).
Go west on US 24 for 2.1 miles to 26th Street. Turn left
(south) on 26th and go 1.4 miles (past the switchback) to
the stop sign (follow signs for Bear Creek Nature Center).
Go straight through the intersection onto Bear Creek Road,
and go 0.2 mile to the Nature Center's parking area, which
is on the left (east).

Key points:
0.3   Reach the Coyote Gulch Trail intersection
1.2   Hook up with the Creekbottom Loop trail

The hike: Interesting questions are posed (and sometimes an-
swered) along the trails surrounding Bear Creek. Will you
see a coyote? Perhaps. A songbird? No doubt. Which wildflowers are in bloom? Maybe you will ponder the sharp de-

lineation of wildland and suburbia on the fringes of the park. Or perhaps your busy mind will be quieted by the easy walking and ample peace that this short loop affords.

Whether you contemplate, meditate or simply ambulate, be sure to visit the Bear Creek Nature Center, located at the trailhead. The displays and dioramas within are extremely well done and offer insight into local ecosystems at levels appropriate for both young children and neophytes, as well as those whose experience in nature is more extensive.

Leave the nature center on the paved trail that heads south. Go left (east) over the bridge that spans the sandy-bottomed creek and pass the start of the Mountain Scrub Loop and Songbird Trail, continuing straight on the pavement. After you pass the second Songbird Trail marker, the path turns to dirt. Interpretive signs line the route. Pass the Nature Trail sign on the right, continuing straight (east). At the next trail crossing, go up and right (south).

Take a breather on the bench at the following trail intersection, then go left (southwest) onto the Coyote Gulch Trail (0.3 mile). At the next trail junction, go left again (southeast). Views open toward the high plains as you climb.

The trail skirts an open, yucca-dotted meadow. Pass a nature trail checkpoint and drop into a gully. The views melt away in the hush of the oak-choked draw.

You'll emerge from the gulch, which is separated from homes by a scrubby greenbelt, into the silvery green of the high grasslands. The trail arcs north, and past a nature trail sign to a trail fork. Go right (downhill/north). At the bench and big juniper, go left on the Creekbottom Loop (1.2 miles).

Drop down a staircase into a bower of oak. The sounds

of Bear Creek rush up at you as you descend. Cross a series of wooden bridges; at the trail crossing, go left (straight/east). Wander through the shady riparian area along the creek to the trailhead and parking area.

Options: As indicated in the trail description, a number of trails crisscross Bear Creek Regional Park. This loop is about the longest; though by addition or subtraction, hikes can be customized for any ability or desire.

Coyote Gulch/Creekbottom Loop

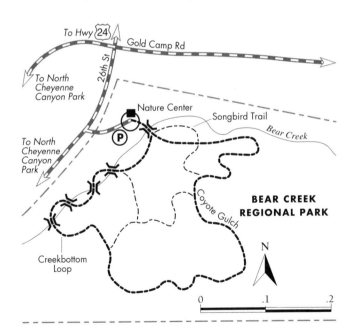

10
FOUNTAIN CREEK TRAIL

Type of hike: Out-and-back.
Total distance: 1.6 miles.
Elevation gain: Minimal.
Maps: USGS Fountain, El Paso County Regional Parks pamphlet.
Starting point: Fountain Creek Regional Park at Willow Springs Road.
Finding the trailhead: Take Interstate 25 south from Colorado Springs to the Security/Widefield and Colorado Highway 16 exit (Exit 132). Go left (east) at the light on CO 16 and drive 0.7 mile to U.S. Highways 85/87. Turn right (south) on US 85/87, and right again immediately onto Willow Springs Road. Parking is 0.4 mile ahead on Willow Springs Road.

Key points:
0.5   Reach the Cattail Marsh Wildlife Area
1.1   Complete the wildlife loop

The hike: Throughout the brief Colorado summer, thunderstorms roll over Pikes Peak and grow dark and bold above the high plains. Watching the battleship-gray storms billow upward, then burst forth with arcing lightning and echoing thunder is electrifying—and quite safe when viewed from the shelters that line the Fountain Creek Regional Trail.

The shelters actually serve a more formal purpose, offering educational information and viewing platforms from which to watch the amazing variety of waterfowl that congregates on the ponds in the Cattail Marsh Wildlife Area.

Fountain Creek Trail

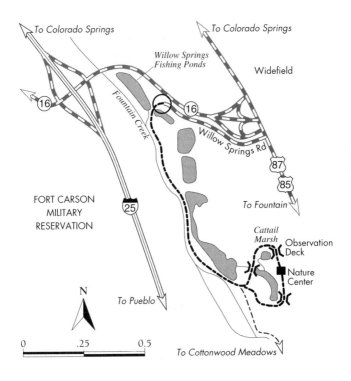

This trail is wide, flat, and easy, sheltered by elegant cottonwoods and elms along Fountain Creek. As well as being wheelchair accessible, the route is shared readily by bicyclists, runners, and walkers. You can start or end your hike with a break at the Willow Springs Fishing Ponds, which offer all the amenities of a good suburban park, including restrooms and a playground.

Begin by walking west from the parking area toward the creek until you reach the wide tree-lined avenue that is the regional trail. Turn left on the broad path and head south. Pass two benches overlooking a pond on the left, as well as an observation deck and educational kiosk. The creek is on the right (west).

The trail veers away from Fountain Creek. Pass a third bench and another interpretive kiosk. Beyond the wildlife observation deck, the trail returns creekside. Reach a fork at a diversion dam. Go left (southeast) onto the trail that explores the Cattail Marsh Wildlife Area (0.5 mile).

This 0.6-mile loop through riparian habitat begins by meandering to the northeast (right) through a meadow ringed by huge trees. At the trail intersection, go left (east), over the bridge between cattail ponds. Beyond another meadow, dense marsh lines both sides of the path. Circle another pond, which sports an observation deck.

Climb briefly to the nature center. On the south side of the building, continue by dropping down the path to another pond. Cross the bridge. At the trail fork, go right (north). The path circumnavigates the meadow to the trail fork at the entrance to the wildlife area. Go left (west), back to the main trail (1.1 mile).

Go right on the Fountain Creek Regional Trail, retracing your steps to the parking area (1.6 miles).

Option: The Fountain Creek Regional Trail continues south from the Cattail Marsh Wildlife Area, offering more opportunities to savor the deep shade of the riparian habitat. You also can walk the flat paths around the Willow Springs Fishing Ponds.

The Mountains

The mountains west of Colorado Springs hold a treasure chest of trails. Each route, like a precious stone, has a different cut, a unique charm, its own sparkle. The Crags Trail, on the shoulder of Pikes Peak, evokes the geode: as you walk on the exposed summit, you can feel the jagged underpinnings that bind the pinnacles to the earth. Other routes circle flawless emerald and sapphire lakes, or climb to the crystalline spill of waterfalls. Still others are chiseled from rock bearing tints of garnet and topaz. Like a shimmering crown, trails encircle the majestic brow of Pikes Peak, patriarch of "the Springs." The trails listed in this section of the guide allow you to share in the dazzle that emanates from these wildlands.

Several small mountain towns offer traditional western amenities, which you can sample before or after hitting the trail. Manitou Springs epitomizes frontier grace; Woodland Park boasts all the modern amenities; and the rural hamlets of Florissant and Divide are quaint but stripped to the necessities—a general store and gas station—like the mountains themselves.

While the hikes venture into steeper terrain, they have this in common: they lie within an hour's drive of Interstate 25, the main artery through Colorado Springs. Directions to trailheads begin at I-25. Hikes are listed from south to north as they would be reached from the interstate, and then from east to west along US Highway 24, which leads from the Springs into the high country.

11
MT. CUTLER TRAIL

Type of hike: Out-and-back.
Total distance: 2 miles.
Elevation gain: 415 feet.
Maps: USGS Colorado Springs and Manitou Springs, Trails Illustrated Pikes Peak/Cañon City.
Starting point: Mt. Cutler trailhead in North Cheyenne Canyon Park.
Finding the trailhead: From Interstate 25, take the Nevada Avenue/Colorado Highway 115 exit (Exit 140B). Go south on Nevada Avenue/CO 115 for about 1 mile and turn right (west) onto Cheyenne Road. Follow Cheyenne Rd. for 2.6 miles to its end at Cheyenne Blvd. (If you approach via Cheyenne Blvd., stay right (west) on Cheyenne Blvd. at this intersection). Go left (west) on Cheyenne Blvd. for 0.1 mile to the Y intersection. Go right (west), through the open gate, into North Cheyenne Canyon Park. The Mt. Cutler trailhead is 1.5 miles up the park road, on the left (south).

Key points:

0.7   Reach the saddle
1.0   The summit is attained

The hike: Given its ecological remoteness, North Cheyenne Canyon Park is astoundingly close to the hubbub of Colo-

Mt. Cutler Trail

rado Springs. A short drive through the charming residential districts of the southwestern section of the city leads to a winding road that climbs up and west into a spectacular preserve of wilderness. From an exposed perch atop Mt. Cutler, you'll enjoy panoramic views of dense forests, the North and South Cheyenne creek drainages, towering red rock formations and a vivid waterfall, as well as vistas of the city and the high plains to the east. The trail is a steady but easy climb, with a thrilling touch of exposure as you traverse the west- and south-facing shoulders of the mountain.

From the trailhead, climb the broad, well-used path through the evergreen forest shading the canyon. Follow upward traverse, crossing slopes littered with deadfall.

The trail flattens briefly at an open area beneath a towering red rock, then arcs through a gully and climbs again. Pass a viewpoint, and a bit beyond, a flat rock that offers good views across the canyon. As you continue the climb, you can see through the portal of the canyon to the high plains beyond.

Reach a saddle with views both west and east (0.7 mile). The trail continues to the left (south and then east), circling the dry backside of the mountain; sparse evergreens cling to the rocky soil. As you continue across the exposed slope, you'll be treated to great views west of Seven Falls.

As the trail nears the end of its circumnavigation of the mountain top, the vistas compete in a delightful battle of one-upmanship. From the summit (1.0 mile), you will enjoy 360-degree views, looking south and east across the high plains and west and north across the backbone of the continent. Return as you came.

Options: North Cheyenne Canyon Park offers an extensive system of trails. On the easy side, there is the short, sweet hike from Helen Hunt Falls to Silver Cascades Falls. Fast and cool, noisy and playful, shot with rainbows and crazy with energy, these twin children of the Cheyenne Canyon creek system exhilarate and beg for attention. You can also challenge yourself on more lengthy (and arduous) treks to Seven Bridges, St. Mary's Fall, and beyond.

Paul Intemann Nature Trail
Lower Barr Trail

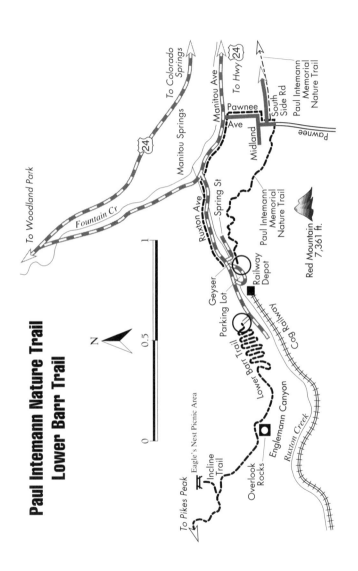

To Woodland Park

To Colorado Springs

Manitou Springs

Fountain Cr

24

Manitou Ave

To Hwy 24

Manitou Ave

Pawnee Ave

Midland

South Side Rd

Paul Intemann Memorial Nature Trail

Pawnee

Ruxton Ave

Spring St

Paul Intemann Memorial Nature Trail

Red Mountain 7,361 ft.

N

Geyser

Railway Depot

Parking Lot

Cog Railway

Lower Barr Trail

Englemann Canyon

Ruxton Creek

Eagle's Nest Picnic Area

Incline Trail

Overlook Rocks

To Pikes Peak

0   0.5   1

12
PAUL INTEMANN NATURE TRAIL

Type of hike: Loop.
Total distance: 3 miles.
Elevation gain: 220 feet.
Maps: USGS Manitou Springs, Trails Illustrated Pikes Peak/Cañon City.
Starting point: Iron Springs Trailhead in Manitou Springs.
Finding the trailhead: To reach the Iron Springs Trailhead, take the Cimarron St./US Hwy. 24 exit from Interstate 25. Follow US 24 west 5.4 miles to the first Manitou Springs exit. The exit ramp circles to Manitou Avenue; turn right, heading west 1.4 miles on Manitou Ave (following the signs for the Cog Railroad). At the intersection of Ruxton Ave. and Manitou Ave., go left (southwest) on Ruxton. Follow Ruxton for 0.7 miles to the Cog Railroad complex. Turn left where the road forks below the depot, and circle around the Iron Springs Chateau. The trailhead is on the right (south), just beyond the private parking area. Park alongside the road.

Key points:
0.5   Traverse at the base of Red Mountain
2.0   Descend Pawnee Avenue
2.5   Reach the Manitou/Ruxton intersection

The hike: This delightful route encompasses all that is wonderful about Colorado. It couples easy hiking through scenic natural areas with a short jaunt through the streets of a classic historic mountain town. Manitou Springs bursts with Victorian quaintness; the homes are well-maintained and the storefronts offer the best of Colorado food, artistry and memorabilia. The town earned fame through its mineral springs; you'll pass one of these just beyond the trailhead.

The trail begins amid the lush growth along Ruxton Creek. Pass percolating Indian Spring Geyser on the left (north). Cross the bridge and link up with Spring Street, turning right (south) as the arrow directs. The route switches back shortly, heading uphill.

Reach and pass a parking area, walking beyond the gate and briefly following a dry wash. Cross the wash just downstream from a concrete dam, and make a short climb to a viewpoint.

The path traverses the sunbaked lower slopes of Red Mountain, alternately flat and uphill (0.5 mile). In a small meadow, look for the sign that points the way eastward. Continue up to another viewpoint; from this trail junction, the main route bends gently right (southeast), briefly flattens, then climbs again.

A lone pine and a power tower mark another viewpoint. At the next trail junction, go left (straight/east), past the sign. Pause at the last vista point before the short descent toward town. You will cross another wash and continue straight (marked with a sign) before the brief drop to Pawnee Ave., which begins as dirt but is soon paved (2 miles).

To continue on the Intemann Trail proper, which leads further east above Manitou Springs, turn right on South Side Road. The loop described here takes you back through town to the trailhead; continue down past an intersection with Midland, staying on Pawnee. At Manitou Ave., go left (west) to Ruxton (2.5 miles). Go left again (uphill and southwest), staying on Ruxton to Spring St. Hook left onto Spring St., then quickly right onto the Intemann Trail, passing the geyser as you return to the trailhead.

13
LOWER BARR TRAIL

see map on page 46

Type of hike: Out-and-back.
Total distance: 6.4 miles.
Elevation gain: 1600 feet.
Maps: USGS Manitou Springs, US Forest Service Pike National Forest Map, Trails Illustrated Pikes Peak/Cañon City.
Starting point: Barr Trailhead in Manitou Springs.
Finding the trailhead: To reach the Barr Trailhead, take the Cimarron St./US Hwy. 24 exit from Interstate 25. Follow US 24 west for 5.4 miles to the first Manitou Springs exit. The exit ramp circles to Manitou Avenue; turn right, heading west 1.4 miles on Manitou Ave (following the signs for the Cog Railroad). At the intersection of Ruxton Ave. and Manitou Ave., go left (southwest) on Ruxton, and follow Ruxton for 0.8 miles, past the Cog Railroad complex, to Hydro Street. Turn right (northwest) on Hydro and go 0.1 mile to the parking area.

Key points:
1.0   Pass the 7200-foot marker
1.8   Rest or turn around at the overlook rocks
2.6   Reach the Incline Trail intersection
3.2   Gaze east from the Eagle's Nest Picnic Area

The hike: Pikes Peak is the ultimate mountain of the Colorado Springs region, and the Barr Trail offers the ultimate hike to the top of this massif. A study in switchbacks, this famous and historic trail climbs an arduous 13 miles and 7400 feet to the summit. Though worthwhile, a hike to the top far exceeds the parameters of this guide. Instead, this short hike on the lower reaches of the trail offers a sample of the terrain, steepness and legend that is Pikes Peak.

This relatively short route features great views and strenuous walking. Wear good shoes, keep a reasonable pace, and if you've the inclination, head on up past the picnic grounds—you'll be amply rewarded.

The trailhead is marked by an informational kiosk. Begin climbing the stairs. Traverse uphill, toward Englemann Canyon, to the next switchback; you will traverse back and forth, ever upward, from westward canyon views to views east to Colorado Springs and the high plains, for the next couple of miles.

At one of the many switchbacks, the trail forks. To visit Ruxton Creek, head straight (left/west) and down the hill. To continue on the Barr Trail, head right (and yes, uphill). Views open northeast to the Garden of the Gods. Eventually, you will pass a switchback with a difference; this one is marked with a sign stating that the summit is 12 miles ahead and the present elevation is 7200 feet (1 mile).

As you continue, the woodland becomes interspersed with large, smooth pieces of granite. The next switchbacks offer granite seats with a spectacular views, and lead to a perch on some spectacular rocks that offer great views over Englemann Canyon (1.8 miles). If you've had enough, this makes a wonderful picnic spot and turn-around point.

If you decide to continue, the path alternately traverses and climbs switchbacks up the south-facing slope of the canyon, gradually bearing west. A rocky ridge slices down between the trail and the route of the cog railroad far below, and a spring feeds a small patch of lush greenery.

Pass through a tunnel made of rocks that have fallen like dominos against each other, then past a "real" tunnel of concrete off to the right (northeast). At 2.6 miles, reach the trail crossing at the top of the incline. Go right (east) on the Incline Trail (the Barr Trail continues to the left).

Follow the flat, wide Incline Trail around to the east to the trail fork just beyond rock cliff. Go left (east) on the less-developed upper trail, heading slightly downhill to the Eagle's Nest Trail sign (3.0 miles). Stay right (east) on the slightly descending trail, which drops to a stunning overlook dotted with weathered picnic tables (3.2 miles). Enjoy an eagle's eye view of Colorado Springs and the plains, which are spread below in a patchwork of green, silver, red and distant gold.

Descend as you came, feasting on great views of the high plains as you return to the trailhead.

14
WALDO CANYON

Type of hike: Loop.
Total distance: 7 miles.
Elevation gain: 1200 feet.
Maps: USGS Manitou Springs, US Forest Service Pike National Forest Map, Trails Illustrated Pikes Peak/Cañon City.
Starting point: Waldo Canyon Trailhead west of Manitou Springs.
Finding the trailhead: To reach the Waldo Canyon Trailhead, take the Cimarron St./US Highway 24 exit from Interstate 25. Follow US 24 west for 7.7 miles to the trailhead parking area on the right (north) side of the highway.

Key points:
1.8   Reach the trail fork at the creek
3.0   Go east at the trail intersection
5.2   Finish the loop at the creek

The hike: Waldo Canyon is the quintessential hike of the mountains west of Colorado Springs. The well-maintained, popular path offers classic views of the pink and gray upper reaches of Pikes Peak and sun-bleached glimpses of the endless expanse of the high plains. The walking is wonderful; you'll warm up by climbing rather steeply on the exposed slopes above the trailhead, then settle into a gentle traverse above the lovely canyon. Beyond, the route plunges into the

Waldo Canyon

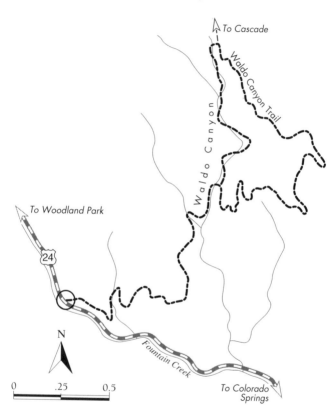

To Cascade

Waldo Canyon Trail

Waldo Canyon

To Woodland Park

24

N

To Colorado Springs

Fountain Creek

0   .25   0.5

riparian shade of a narrow stream, and finally, a descent along south-facing ridges of vivid red leads back to the trailhead. Get to the trailhead early on sunny summer weekends, as the parking lot fills quickly, and bring your own water as there is none potable along the trail.

To begin, climb the stairs, round the switchback and sign the register. Continue the switchbacking climb upward, passing a viewpoint on the right marked with a geological information sign, and a knob with informal trails that branch east to an overlook. The main trail arcs northwest, traversing the open slope toward the head of the valley, which is marked by gray cliffs from which issues a narrow waterfall.

The trail crosses a clear little stream in a shady gully, then enters the meadow on the ledge above the waterfall; a rustic campsite is nestled in the flowering grasses. At 1.8 miles, reach a trail fork and a sign denoting the beginning of the loop trail, which is 3.5 miles long. You can go either way; the route is described here by going left (west), into the forest, across the stream and around a switchback.

Climb gently as the trail laces up the bed of the narrowing creek, crossing the waterway six times (none are serious creek crossings). At 3.0 miles, the creekside ramble ends at a trail intersection above a rough staircase; the Waldo Canyon Trail goes right (east).

The route climbs eastward amid boulders and large evergreens, with great views south across the valley to Pikes Peak. Keep a careful eye to the right (south) side of the trail for a trail sign; when you reach it, the trail immediately switches back to the left (west). If you go straight (and you won't be the only one who has), you'll end up on a rock outcrop with great views but nowhere to go.

Drop down to a creek crossing, then continue to traverse the south-facing slope. The views of Pikes Peak unbelievably become more and more spectacular as you hike; at the interpretive sign about "The Great Non-Conformity," the massif is a perfect picture of Rocky Mountain splendor.

The trail rollercoasters over a ridge top into mountain scrub, with views now of the high plains. Pass a trail sign at a switchback to the right (southeast), and continue the downward traverse, crossing a large red sandstone slab as you descend. Pink slabs lined with scrub lead down along the south-facing slope to another interpretive sign, then a series of switchbacks, ever steepening, lead back to the trail crossing at the beginning of the loop (5.2 miles). From here, you'll retrace your steps back to the trailhead parking area.

15
CATAMOUNT FALLS TRAIL

Type of hike: Loop.
Total distance: 2 miles.
Elevation gain: 377 feet.
Maps: USGS Cascade, US Forest Service Pike National Forest Map, Trails Illustrated Pikes Peak/Cañon City.
Starting point: Lake Street trailhead in Green Mountain Falls.
Finding the trailhead: Take the Cimarron St./US Highway 24 exit from Interstate 25. Follow US 24 west 15.5 miles to the second Green Mountain Falls exit. Go left (south, then east) onto Ute Pass Avenue, following it 0.7 mile to Lake Street. Park in the public lot; this is the trailhead.

Key points:
0.7   Belvidere Avenue ends
1.0   Reach the falls
1.5   Descend Hondo Avenue

The hike: Every step you take along the Catamount Falls Trail transports you to a simpler time. This is one of three historic trails maintained with pride by the tiny town of Green Mountain Falls, which calls itself "The Gem of the Rockies." The charm of the old town and its trails is subtle and quaint—and not at all limited to the wonders of its natural setting. A gingerbread gazebo sits on an island in the small lake at the trailhead; splendid examples of Western frontier architecture overlook the route; rustic summer cabins and well-kept private residences line the narrow, winding avenues. The steep, tumbling falls themselves, reached via a rustic trail that once was made by ladies wearing Victorian gowns and carrying parasols, are a refreshing midpoint on this delightful route.

Begin by walking right (west) from the kiosk. Take Ute Pass Avenue right (west), past Oak Avenue and Maple Street. A shady park lies by Catamount Creek. Cross Ute Pass Ave. as you turn left (west) onto Belvidere Avenue.

A steady gentle climb on Belvidere leads past charming cottages and mountain cabins. Stay on Belvidere, ignoring side streets. Beyond the Midland Avenue intersection, the road steepens a bit.

After about 0.7 mile, the road deadends at a gate. A sign here describes how, in 1887, the general manger of Green Mountain Falls Town and Improvement Co. named the village after the falls on Crystal and Catamount Creeks. Go left (south), past the gate, and continue on the dirt road into the woods.

A water tank comes into view as the trail flattens. Reach the bridge over Catamount Creek; the cataract tumbles above and below the bridge. The rough, steep path to the falls proper begins to the right of the cascade. Climb alongside the falls and enjoy the cooling spray (1 mile).

After enjoying the falls, return to the bridge and water tank. Go right (northeast), over the bridge, and down the dirt road (Hondo Avenue).

As you descend on Hondo (1.5 miles), you'll pass a fire gate and several side streets. Just past Howard Street, take

Catamount Falls Trail

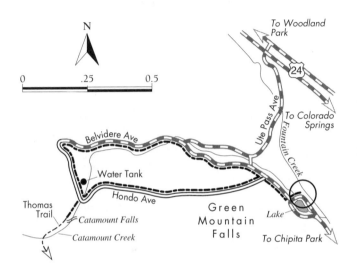

the right fork to Ute Pass Ave. Cross the street and turn right (east), retracing your steps to the trailhead.

Options: You can continue on the trail that climbs along the falls, called the Thomas Trail, to Crystal Falls for a three-mile loop trip through the woods above Green Mountain Falls. Or, you can hike 1 mile to Crystal Falls directly via Hotel, Park and Boulder streets, returning on Mountain and Foster Avenues. Check out the map at the trailhead, which shows the options.

Rainbow Gulch
BPW Nature Trail

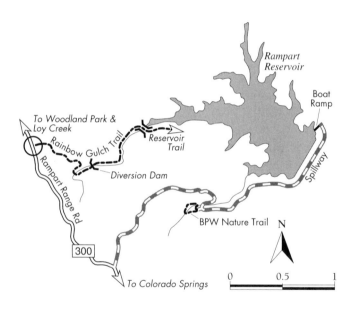

Rampart
Reservoir

Boat
Ramp

To Woodland Park &
Loy Creek

Rainbow Gulch Trail

Reservoir
Trail

Spillway

Diversion Dam

Rampart Range Rd

BPW Nature Trail

N

300

To Colorado Springs

0   0.5   1

16
RAINBOW GULCH

Type of hike: Out-and-back.

Total distance: 2.5 miles.

Elevation gain: 180 feet.

Maps: USGS Cascade, US Forest Service Pike National Forest Map, Trails Illustrated Pikes Peak/Cañon City.

Starting point: Rainbow Gulch Trailhead in the Rampart Reservoir Recreation Area.

Finding the trailhead: Take the Cimarron St./US Highway 24 exit from Interstate 25. Follow US 24 west about 18 miles to Woodland Park. Turn right (northwest) on Baldwin Street (at the Welcome to Woodland Park sign). Follow Baldwin through three stop signs; it becomes Rampart Range Road and leads 2.9 miles to Loy Creek Road. Turn right (northeast) on Loy Creek, following the sign for Rampart Reservoir, and drive 1.5 miles to the next intersection. Go right (southeast) on Rampart Range Road (Forest Service Road 300); there is another sign. Drive 2.4 miles to the Rainbow Gulch Trailhead and parking area on the left (north).

Key points:

0.5   Pass the diversion dam

1.0   Cross the bridge near the lake shore

The hike: The inky depths of Rampart Reservoir are clasped in the ancient rock and forest of Pikes Peak's north slope.

One of the most scenic lakes in Colorado's foothills, the slender fingers of the reservoir sprawl into a number of stream-carved draws. Lovely Rainbow Gulch is one of these.

The gulch trail slips gently down along the stream to the shores of the lake, where it joins the well-used trail system encircling the reservoir. In addition to superb hiking, the recreation area offers a plethora of outdoor fun, including great fishing and mountain biking.

From the parking area, head down on the dirt track through aspen, evergreens and boulders. Round a bend and continue the gentle descent, following a ramshackle fence. Just beyond the narrow meadow, the walls of the gulch close in on the trail.

The trail flattens amid a graveyard of evergreens, then drops again and switches back over a stream. Pass a big, mossy boulder as you continue. At the trail fork atop the diversion dam, stay left (northwest). Willows encroach on the water's edge; the stream, in its well-defined rock-lined banks, is a rip-roaring hiking companion (0.5 mile).

The broad trail meanders at streamside for another half-mile, lazing through intermittent woodland and meadow. At 1.0 mile, reach a bridge over the stream; the reservoir is deep blue in the near distance. Cross the bridge to the trail on the other side of the stream, and go left (north) toward the lake. At the trail fork stay left, shadowing the waterway.

The gravel-strewn mouth of the stream empties into a spidery arm of the reservoir. The path climbs briefly to intersect the 11-mile trail around the reservoir. You can continue on the reservoir trail if you've the time. Otherwise, climb back to the trailhead by the same route (2.5 miles).

17
BPW NATURE TRAIL

see map on page 60

Type of hike: Loop.
Total distance: 1 mile.
Elevation gain: Minimal.
Maps: USGS Cascade, US Forest Service Pike National Forest Map, Trails Illustrated Pikes Peak/Cañon City.
Starting point: BPW Trailhead in the Rampart Reservoir Recreation Area.
Finding the trailhead: From Interstate 25, take the Cimarron St./US Highway 24 exit. Follow US 24 west about 18 miles to Woodland Park. Turn right (northwest) on Baldwin Street (at the Welcome to Woodland Park sign). Follow Baldwin through three stop signs; it becomes Rampart Range Road and leads 2.9 miles to Loy Creek Road. Turn right (northeast) on Loy Creek, following the sign for Rampart Reservoir, and drive 1.5 miles to the next intersection. Go right (southeast) on Rampart Range Road (Forest Service Road 300); there is another sign. Drive 3.8 miles to a left turn onto a paved road. This leads 0.5 mile north to the Rampart Reservoir entrance station; there is a small fee. From the station, follow the reservoir road for 0.8 mile to the BPW Nature Trail parking area on the right side of the road.

Key points:
0.5   Pass the small tunnel in the creek
0.8   Traverse the shady north-facing slope

The hike: This short, delightful romp through an old-growth aspen woodland on the slopes above Rampart Reservoir is perfect for children and those seeking a lesson in the nature of the Rocky Mountains. A number of interpretive signs line the narrow trail, offering short lessons on mountain ecology, including the nature of the fauna and the conditions that produce the varying ecosystems.

Restrooms are provided at the trailhead. Descend to the little foot bridge and cross it, climbing gently through old-growth aspen. You'll pass several switchbacks and interpretive signs about such varied topics as ponderosa pines and gophers as the trail meanders through woodland and meadow.

Reach a bench nestled among glacial "erratics," the huge boulders forming a small cave adjacent to the trail. More interpretive signs border the wooden walkway; the trail snakes to the creekside, where a bench invites you to sit and watch the water tumble over a small ledge and through a delightful miniature tunnel (0.5 mile).

Cross the boardwalk to the next interpretive sign. The trail hooks back toward the trailhead, following the bed of the stream. Pass two more signs as the trail follows the shady north-facing slope; this section can be soggy in spring (0.8 mile). A short distance farther, and the trail leads back into the parking area.

18
MANITOU PARK LAKE

Type of hike: Loop.
Total distance: 1 mile.
Elevation gain: Minimal.
Maps: USGS Mount Deception, US Forest Service Pike National Forest Map, Trails Illustrated Pikes Peak/Cañon City topo map.
Starting point: Manitou Park Lake picnic area.
Finding the trailhead: Take the Cimarron St./US Highway 24 exit from Interstate 25. Follow US 24 west about 18 miles to its intersection with Colorado Highway 67 in Woodland Park. Turn right (north) on CO 67 and follow this 7.8 miles to Manitou Park Lake. Turn right (east); park in the first or second lot. A fee is levied for use of this Forest-Service maintained area.

Key points:
0.1   Walk atop the dam
0.5   Reach the trail fork
0.7   Cross the boardwalks through the marsh

The hike: Easy to reach and easy to enjoy, little Manitou Park Lake is a pleasant diversion from the rigors of the high country. Little more than a stroll, this short hike allows visitors ample opportunity to view the stark north face of Pikes Peak, and to picnic and fish in an alpine setting.

The willowy wetlands along the south shore of the lake, transected by snaking Trout Creek, harbor a variety of songbirds and waterfowl, as well as wildflowers and shrubbery that blooms in abundant and colorful profusion in spring and early summer.

The trail begins at the north end of the lake. Begin by crossing the bridge, from which you can watch the water tumble down the spillway, or look south to the steely sum-

Manitou Park Lake

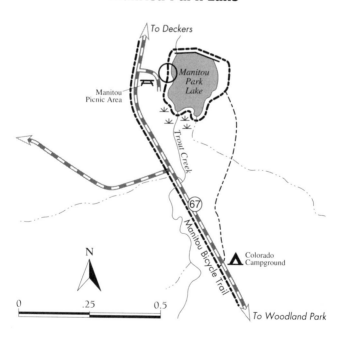

mit of Pikes Peak. On the other side of the bridge, stairs lead to lakeside on the south (right), and creekside on the north (left). Continue by walking atop the earthen dam.

The trail forks at the end of the dam (0.1 mile). The low road (which can be wet in spring and early summer) stays by the lake and offers access for fishermen. Take the high road (left/straight) up and around the knoll.

You will pass through a grove of shady conifers, then through more lush meadow, which drops gently to the friendly bottle-green lake. Mountain aster, Indian paintbrush and willows decorate the lake shore through most of the hiking season.

At the next trail fork (0.5 mile), go straight (right/south-west) on the trail bordering the lake. Pass a bench at the onset of the marsh that crowds the southern reaches of the water. The trail drops onto a boardwalk through head-high cattails. An interpretive sign describes the functions of a wetland. Cross the inlet streams, passing another interpre-tive sign (0.7 mile).

The boardwalk ends beyond the third interpretive dis-play and the trail climbs gently along the west shore of the lake into the picnic area. A short hop through the shade of ponderosa pines leads back to the bridge and trailhead (1 mile).

Option: If you'd like to make the hike a bit longer, go left (south) at the trail fork just before you enter the marsh, con-tinuing up through the meadow. The path runs alongside the fenced boundary of the Colorado Campground to CO 67. Cross the road and turn right (north), heading back to the lake via the paved Manitou Bicycle Trail.

19
OUTLOOK RIDGE AND LOST POND LOOP

Type of hike: Loop.
Total distance: 2.9 miles.
Elevation loss/gain: 280 feet.
Maps: USGS Divide, Mueller State Park and Wildlife Area trail map, Trails Illustrated Pikes Peak/Cañon City topo map.
Starting point: Outlook Ridge Trailhead in Mueller State Park and Wildlife Area.
Finding the trailhead: Take the Cimarron St./US Highway 24 exit from Interstate 25. Follow US 24 west about 18 miles to its intersection with Colorado Highway 67 in Woodland Park. Continue straight (southwest) on US 24/CO 67 for 6.4 miles to the town of Divide. Turn left (south) on CO 67; go 3.8 miles to the park entrance (there is a fee). Turn right (west), following Wapiti Road 1.5 miles to the Outlook Ridge parking area on the left (south).

Key points:
0.6   Walk out to the Raven Ridge Overlook
1.5   Check out the views from the Lone Eagle Overlook
2.3   Pass Lost Pond

The hike: Just as a well-designed museum is the perfect forum for displays of fine art, Mueller State Park and Wild-

Outlook Ridge and Lost Pond Loop

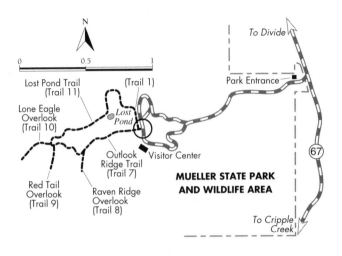

life Area is an unsurpassed showcase for the natural wonders of Colorado's high country. Rock outcrops on the Outlook Ridge Trail offer picture-perfect views of the gray and green ramparts of Pikes Peak, as well as of the high valleys spreading west from its summit. Views are curtailed by silent forest on the second half of the hike—a vital woodland that tints the sunlight a pale shade of green. Lost Pond is secluded and bucolic, a small watering hole for deer and songbirds ringed in waist-high grasses and wildflowers for most of the hiking season.

Mueller State Park's seclusion renders it virtually immune to overcrowding, ensuring peace and isolation. The trail system within the park is extensive, and this loop can be tied into others to either lengthen or shorten the hike. The loop described below is marked by blue arrows, but feel free to explore and enjoy.

Begin by passing the restrooms and picnic areas. At the intersection with Lost Pond Trail, stay left (straight/west) on Outlook Ridge Trail (Trail 7). The trail dips in and out of a swale, passing trail signs.

Detour to the left (south) on Raven Ridge (Trail 8). This short side trip offers great views of Pikes Peak and the rugged mountains to the south. Return to the main trail and go left (west), heading down through aspen (0.6 mile).

Unless you are tempted, pass the Red Tail Overlook trail. Another succulent overlook will be served up shortly. That overlook trail, called Lone Eagle (Trail 10), lies at an intersection marked by a bench. Go left (up/west) and rollercoaster along the fence to the vantage point (1.5 miles).

After feasting on the spectacular views west from the overlook, return to the main trail. Go left and up (east), following the blue arrows. At the crest of the hill the old roadbed flattens, then plunges down into a wooded draw. Cross the creek, and climb steeply out of the drainage. From the top of a short, steep ascent, the trail (Trail 11) traverses above the hollow, which deepens into shadow below.

The rustic roadbed narrows to single track in a swampy area as it approaches Lost Pond. The pond lies tucked in a lovely pocket of forest and meadow; look for waterfowl and blooming water lilies, depending on the season (2.3 miles).

Leave the pond by climbing northward up to the head of the valley; the trail then circles east toward the road. At the trail signs, go left, up the short staircase. Go past the staircase for about 100 feet and turn right (south) on Trail 1. Follow this trail for 0.5 mile until it intersects the Outlook Ridge Trail, and walk back through the picnic area to the trailhead (2.9 miles).

20
THE CRAGS

Type of hike: Out-and-back.
Total distance: 4 miles.
Elevation gain: 500 feet.
Maps: USGS Pikes Peak and Woodland Park, US Forest Service Pike National Forest Map, Trails Illustrated Pikes Peak/Cañon City topo map.
Starting point: The Crags Trailhead in Crags Campground.
Finding the trailhead: Take the Cimarron St./US Highway 24 exit from Interstate 25. Follow US 24 west for about 18 miles to Colorado Highway 67 in Woodland Park. Go left (southwest) on US 24/CO 67 for 6.4 miles to the town of Divide, where the highways diverge. Turn left (south) on CO 67, and go 4.1 miles to a left turn marked with a Crags Campground sign (Teller Co. Road 62). Follow this dirt road 1.5 miles east to the Rocky Mountain Mennonite Camp, and go right (south). The rough road leads another 1.5 miles to the Crags Campground. Go left (east), and follow the campground road until it ends in a small parking lot at the trailhead.

Key points:
1.2   Cross the log foot bridge
1.7   Reach the saddle
2.0   Enjoy the views from the summit

The hike: Want that top-of-the-mountain experience without actually conquering a massive peak? Then hike to The Crags and rejoice.

The trail to these jagged summits has all the exposure, solitude, and views that a full-fledged mountain climb does, but the thighs and lungs won't feel the burn like they would on neighboring Pikes Peak. Don't be misled, however; this hike has its challenges, including a steady climb and a difficult-to-discern trail toward the summit. Though the trail is not technically difficult, good hiking shoes, good route-finding skills and gumption will ensure good fun.

From the parking area, the trail passes the pump and picnic table, then parallels Fourmile Creek, which spills through its bed below and to the right. Pass what looks like the cover of a cistern, then enter a lovely meadow with great views up the valley.

The trail gets more rustic as it skirts the lush meadows. You will enjoy dominating views of the barren shoulder of Pikes Peak before aspens and evergreens crowd the trail at about the half-mile point.

Climb gently away from the creek, cresting a small hill before hiking into another stunning meadow. Soggy logs provide purchase through a willowy wet area. An extravaganza of early summer wildflowers and tall rock outcrops decorate the trail for the next half mile, leading to a log bridge that crosses the stream. Stay right on the main path (1.2 mile).

You'll climb in earnest as the trail narrows into a wooded gully. An ascending series of roots and water bars mark the

The Crags

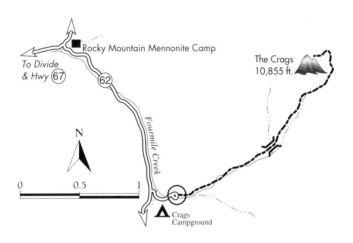

route, but stay alert. The forest floor is relatively devoid of cluttering undergrowth, leaving the remote potential that you could stray from the trail.

Reach a saddle. The trail veers left (north), dipping briefly before climbing over fallen logs to a viewpoint. A huge rusty crag looms to the east (1.7 miles). From here, the trail continues up and left (north, then west) onto the open ridge. Drift right onto the huge slab for 360-degree views, then continue up the orange-earth trail to the summit area. Though wide and flat, it drops precipitously at the edges, so watch yourself and your children (2 miles).

And savor the views. Pikes Peak is an imposing presence on the south side, its massive rocky shoulder hulking above. To the west and north, the mountains roll away to the horizon, skirted in rich deep green and crowned with silver. To the east, beyond the lapis Catamount reservoirs, the mountains diminish until they are flattened in the hazy gold of the high plains.

Return as you came, taking care to remain on the trail as you descend through the wooded gully.

21
HORSETHIEF FALLS

Type of hike: Out-and-back.
Total distance: 3 miles.
Elevation gain: 500 feet.
Maps: USGS Cripple Creek North and Pikes Peak, US Forest Service Pike National Forest Map, Trails Illustrated Pikes Peak/Cañon City topo map.
Starting point: Horsethief Falls Trailhead off Colorado Highway 67 at the Waters Tunnel.
Finding the trailhead: To reach the trailhead, take the Cimarron St./US Highway 24 exit from Interstate 25. Follow US 24 west for about 18 miles to its intersection with Colorado Highway 67 in Woodland Park. Go left (south and west) on US 24/CO 67 for 6.4 miles to the town of Divide, where the highways diverge. Turn left (south) on CO 67, and go about 9 miles to the summit of the pass. The parking area is on the left (east) just beyond the summit; the closed Waters Tunnel marks the spot.

Key points:
0.8   The steep climb ends
1.0   Pass the trail sign
1.5   Rest beside Horsethief Falls

The hike: In the shady depths of the evergreen forest, a steep, relentless climb leads into a secluded park, where a crystalline waterfall spills over a jumble of rocks. The cataract plays a muted symphony on the lichen-stained stone, a gentle destination for the hiker who seeks tranquility.

The hike to Horsethief Falls is not entirely easy, as about 300 feet are gained quickly and without a mitigating switchback. Once in Horsethief Park, however, the path is a scenic delight, meandering through trees that part for views of aspen groves, wildflowers, and the gray bulk of Pikes Peak.

The trail departs from the right (south) end of the trailhead parking area, climbing above the highway. Round a switchback at the fence, and continue up, traversing above the tunnel. At the barricade, go right (east) and—you guessed it—up.

Horsethief Falls

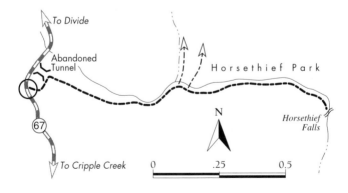

Around the next bend the sound of water rushing in the valley below overtakes the noise of the highway. This distant melody accompanies you as you sweat up the steep track. Rocks litter the trail just before it flattens, blissfully, alongside the stream (0.8 mile).

At the two trail forks above the steep section, stay to the right, veering slightly southeast and keeping to the south side of the creek. Pass the trail sign at the entrance to Horsethief Park. The path continues climbing gently through open woodland, with the willow-cloaked stream on the left (north) and sloping meadow beyond. Aspens cluster and quake on the high slopes above the quiet stream. At the next trail sign, go left, across the streamlet and into the meadow, following the arrow; from here, it is a half-mile to the falls (1 mile).

A scar of red earth flickers in and out of view as you climb into the woods. The trail runs streamside to the base of the cataract (1.5 miles). You can cross the logs over the stream to rest on the rocks on the north side, or skirt the hillside to a perch on south side. Either way, the sunlight is filtered through the canopy of evergreen boughs, warming spots for picnics or naps.

Return as you came—it's all downhill from the falls.

22

PETRIFIED FOREST TRAIL/ WALK THROUGH TIME TRAIL

Type of hike: Two loops.
Total distance: 1.5 miles.
Elevation gain: 50 feet.
Maps: USGS Lake George, Trails Illustrated Pikes Peak/ Cañon City topo map.
Jurisdiction: Florissant Fossil Beds National Monument.
Starting point: Monument Visitor Center.
Finding the trailhead: To reach the trailheads, take the Cimarron St./US Highway 24 exit from Interstate 25. Follow US 24 west for 35 miles, passing through Woodland Park and Divide, to the town of Florissant. Turn left (south) on Teller County Highway 1 (a Scenic Byway), and drive 2 miles to the visitor center road. Turn right (west) and go 0.2 mile to the parking area. There is a small fee.

Key points:
0.3   Start the Petrified Forest loop
1.0   Finish the loop by the visitor center
1.5   Complete A Walk Through Time Trail

The hike: They hunker in fields of bleached meadow grasses and on the fringes of a more youthful forest—abbreviated towers of multicolored stone that speak eloquently of the grandeur that once was. They are the petrified stumps of giant sequoias that were buried by mudflows that also dammed the valley and created Lake Florissant.

These ancient trees were preserved by volcanic mudflows; the minerals in the mud gradually petrified the wood, preserving it for the enjoyment and edification of today's visitors. These guided walks are delightfully easy, the perfect getaway for families. Longer hikes within the monument are available; pick up a brochure at the visitor center.

You will start out on A Walk Through Time Trail, which begins behind the visitor center on the paved path. Pick up the guide, which describes what you will see at each of the numbered posts along the route. Shortly, you'll pass the first petrified sequoia stump. At post 2, go right to visit the yurts, one of which houses a single huge stump, and the other a cluster of three. Return to the main trail and go left on the gravel path, through the ponderosa-studded grasslands.

Just past marker 3, the trail forks. Go right on the Petrified Forest Loop (picking up the second trail guide, if you choose). Pass markers 1 and 2 in the woods (0.3 mile).

Beyond marker 3 and a dead ponderosa, the trail veers right and down. Pass a bench overlooking the ancient lakebed and marker 4. Pass a huge, gorgeous, multicolored stump, a bench, and marker 5 before the trail turns right (east) and heads across the meadow. Climb gently around a hillock and check out markers 6 through 10 as you circle through the grasses. A series of signs making up a timeline leads back to the visitor center and trailhead (1 mile).

To complete A Walk Through Time nature trail, pass the visitor center and yurts to the trail intersection with the

Petrified Forest Trail/
Walk Through Time Trail

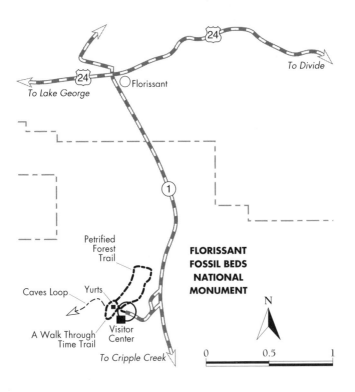

Petrified Forest Loop, and turn left (west). Climb past interpretive markers to the Caves Loop intersection; go left, staying on A Walk Through Time Trail. The trail markers pass in quick succession, yielding a wealth of information about the past and present ecoystems of the area. The trail ends at marker 16; the visitor center and parking area are just beyond (1.5 miles). Return the trail guides for other visitors to use, or you may purchase one for a nominal fee.

About the Author

Tracy Salcedo has been an writer and outdoors enthusiast for most of her life. She is the author of ten *12 Short Hikes* guidebooks to Colorado, where she was a resident for 12 years. In addition, she has written numerous articles on hiking, mountain biking and skiing for Colorado newspapers and several national magazines. She currently resides in California's Wine Country, where, in the company of her husband and three sons, she continues her writing and outdoor pursuits.

Another Hike in Colorado!

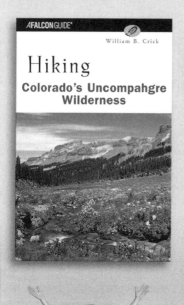

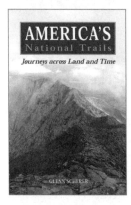
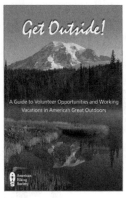